Dos Mundos
Two Worlds

A Journey Through Color, Conflict, and Unity

Written By

James Bass

CLARICE JEFFERIES

Dos Mundos / Two Worlds

A Journey Through Color, Conflict, and Unity

by James Bass

Published by Clarice Jefferies Publishing

Contact info: cjpublishing@yahoo.com

Copyright © 2025 James Bass

CLARICE JEFFERIES

TABLE OF CONTENTS

Born Between Borders: *Early childhood memories of love from Abuelita, racial slurs from neighbors, and being seen as " other" in both communities*

The Darker the Hue, the Deeper the Pain:
Deep dive into colorism from both sides: Abuelita's warmth vs. mother's shame; being darker than even some full-blooded Mexicans

When Home Feels Like Hostile Ground: *Violent abuse from Sid and Rock, being punished for being "Black," learning shame in your own skin*

Pretty Boy and the Broken Mirror: *Catechism violence, being isolated and bullied in church, culminating in stabbing a peer—rage birthed by rejection*

My Mother, the Mirror, and Her Lies: *Living with a Mexican mother who hates Blackness—unpacking inherited hate and generational trauma*

Brown and Black: A Love Letter to Unity: *The dream of solidarity: what could be if the war between these communities ended*

Legacy of a Dual-Blooded Man: *Final reflections on identity, hope, healing, and passing down a new path for the next generation*

DEDICATION

*For my Abuela, Esperanza Armas—whose name means hope,
and who was hope when the world offered me none.*

*Thank you for loving me when others only saw my darkness.
For holding me with arms stronger than silence, and for seeing
beauty in the skin I was taught to be ashamed of.*

*You fed me when I was hungry—for food, for safety, for love.
You defended me when even blood turned its back. You never tried
to change me. You never turned away.*

You were the first place I felt like I belonged.

*Everything I am, everything I survived, and everything I'm
still becoming—began in your kitchen, in your prayers, in your
unwavering love.*

Your legacy lives.

Te amo, Abuelita. Siempre.

PREFACE

I didn't write this book to be liked...

I wrote it because it was the only way I survived.

For most of my life, I've been stuck between two worlds—Black and Mexican. I was born into both, shaped by both, and nearly destroyed by both. In one world, I was a *mayate*—too dark, too foreign, too "other." In the other, I was *not Black enough*—too light, too Spanish, too soft. I was never fully embraced. Never truly at home.

And yet, I *am* both.

This is not a story of blame. It's a story of becoming. Becoming a man in the absence of love. Becoming visible after being erased. Becoming whole after growing up fractured by colorism, violence, rejection, and silence. This is about navigating the war between two cultures that live in my blood—and the possibility of what could happen if those two cultures ever chose unity over division.

I tell this story because I lived every minute of it—from the bruises to the corner punishments, from attempted suicides to accidental survival, from rage to redemption. Every chapter is a scar. Every reflection is a step toward healing. This is not fiction. This is a reckoning.

You'll meet my mother—a Mexican woman whose shame burned through her like wildfire.

You'll meet the men who beat me, tortured me, belittled me, left me.

You'll meet my Abuelita—my saving grace, my angel.

You'll walk with me through classrooms that failed me, churches that judged me, and gangs that turned on me because I didn't fit the mold.

And then, you'll witness something more important than any of that: **the decision to live anyway.**

This book isn't just about pain. It's about power—the kind you reclaim when you choose to break cycles instead of repeating them. When you choose to love your partner openly. When you choose to speak your truth, even when your voice shakes.

For every mixed child who's ever asked, "Where do I belong?"

For every Black man who grew up without a father.

For every Brown girl who was told her skin was too dark to be beautiful.

For every soul who's been called *too much* or *not enough*—

This book is for you.

Not as a blueprint... But as proof.

Proof that survival is possible...

That healing is possible...

That unity is possible...

And that your story—no matter how complicated, how painful, how unfinished—is still yours to write.

This is mine.

And I offer it to you, unfiltered and unflinching, because we deserve to tell the truth...

We deserve to heal...

We deserve to be whole.

James—Jaime

A Dual-Blooded Man

Chapter 1:
Born Between Borders

I was born in 1974, between two fires that never stopped burning. On one side, the rhythmic, grounded strength of my **Black heritage**—deep, proud, ancient. On the other, the passionate, complex layers of my **Mexican blood**—vibrant, wounded, and loud with tradition. I am both. But in the eyes of the world I grew up in, I was neither enough to be one nor accepted fully by the other.

The first time I heard the word "mayate," (nigger) I was four years old. A group of Mexican adults, brown as molasses and just as sun-scorched as my own skin, hurled it at me and my Abuelita as we walked to the grocery market. They spit at us, not metaphorically, but literally, their saliva flying through the hot Fresno, California air to mark us like enemies. My Abuelita clutched me tight and shielded my face with her blouse. She didn't flinch. She never flinched. Her name was Esperanza, which means "hope," and that's exactly what she gave me. Even as the venom rained down, she whispered to me softly, "They are broken, not you."

What they couldn't see was that the little boy they were spitting at was their blood, too. My mother was Mexican-American, born right here in California. But because my father was Black, because my skin bore his features more than hers, I was erased from the category of "ours" and placed into the abyss of "them." Not light enough to be Mexican, not connected enough to be Black...

But just Black enough to be hated.

When you're born into a body that makes you a battlefield, every mirror is a line in the sand. As a child, I'd look at myself and try to piece together which half of me deserved to exist more. My curls were tight, not loose like the high-yellow cousins my mother adored.

My skin was deep brown, not bronze like the light-skinned Afro-Mexicans on Univision. Even my Spanish felt questioned—like a thief wearing someone else's name.

But Abuelita never questioned me. She cooked chorizo con huevos and sang to me on Saturday mornings while Radio Bilingüe played in the background. I watched her make tortillas from scratch and how to make menudo with love. When I cried because the kids in catechism called me "mayate" or refused to sit next to me during prayer, she held me like I was the most precious child in the world. I can still hear her saying, *"No estás solo, Jaimito. Nunca estás solo."* You are not alone, James. Never alone.

She was the only one who gave me that feeling—of being seen without needing to be edited. Everyone else wanted me to shrink. To fade. My mother, for example, never missed an opportunity to let me know how much she resented having a Black child. Her words cut deeper than any schoolyard insult. When we passed Black men in the street, she'd call them "sorry ass niggers" like it was her native language. When she was angry with me, she'd use the same word, only this time laced with maternal venom: "You're going to grow up to be just like your sorry-ass nigger daddy."

I didn't know what hate was until I saw it behind my mother's eyes. And I didn't know what shame was until I realized that I shared the same face as the people she taught me to distrust.

What saved me, oddly, were the contradictions. My Mexican side called me "mayate," but my Mexican grandmother loved me unconditionally. My Black side was absent—my father left me nothing but skin and silence but the kids at school still reminded me I was one of "them." It was as if the world had decided that being both meant belonging to no one.

But I belonged to Abuelita.

We'd often talk about race, but she showed me love through her actions—through frijoles and freshly swept floors, through hand-sewn clothes and long walks to the store. **When the world made me feel dirty for being dark, she'd wash me clean with her adoration.**

She never explained why the world hated me. Maybe she didn't know. Or maybe she knew too well and wanted to protect me from understanding it too early.

Still, even her love couldn't keep the world from getting in. By the time I was eight, I had already developed a rage I couldn't name. I fought other kids not because I was tough, but out of necessity. It was the only time I felt seen. Even if they feared me, at least they saw me.

And somewhere in the middle of all that chaos—between violence at home and hatred in the streets—I began to ask myself: ***What would happen if Black and Brown people stopped hating each other? What if the love my Abuelita gave me could be the rule and not the rare exception? What if unity wasn't a dream, but a weapon? A revolution?***

That question stayed with me like a splinter in my soul. Because what I knew even back then was this: **if Black and Brown ever stopped fighting and started building— truly building together—the world would never be the same.**

But unity was hard to imagine when my own reflection still made me sick.

I didn't know then how much more pain was waiting for me. I didn't know how many beatings, betrayals, and breakdowns I'd survive. But I did know this: **being born between borders wasn't a curse. It was a calling. One I would spend the rest of my life answering.**

Chapter 2:

THE DARKER THE HUE, THE DEEPER THE PAIN

Color isn't just something you see. It's something you feel, especially when it's weaponized against you. And when you're born dark in a light-skinned family, color becomes a language. A hierarchy. A knife disguised as a compliment or a subtle silence at the dinner table.

Growing up, I didn't just feel Black—I felt *too* Black. Too dark for the family portraits. Too dark to get the "mijo" (son) hugs from my mother. Too dark to sit in the front seat during holidays. It wasn't ever said outright, but it was always understood: my skin made my mother uncomfortable, even when my blood matched hers.

Colorism doesn't shout. It whispers. It's the way my lighter-skinned cousins got kissed first, picked first, celebrated more. It's the way certain family members would tell them how handsome they were, while only commenting on how "strong" I looked— like I was some field hand from the 1800s. The message was clear: light was beauty... light was love... light was safety...

And I was not.

Even the mirrors in my house seemed to betray me. I used to study my face, looking for evidence that I could belong. I'd pull at my hair, try to flatten it, curl my lips in ways that looked more "Mexican." I wanted to be small and light-skinned with soft, manageable hair and light eyes like my cousin Joe. He got "You look just like a movie star." I got "You better behave, or the police will come for you."

No matter how "Mexican" my culture was—how much Spanish I spoke, how many tortillas I rolled, how many Our Fathers I prayed in a church filled with white Jesuses—I could never wash off my Blackness. And even when I tried to lean into it, I found that my "Black card" came with conditions, too.

When I did cross paths with other Black kids, many didn't accept me either. "You talk like a white boy," they'd say. I didn't have the cultural rhythm, the slang, the deep generational bonds. They'd look at me and say, "You ain't Black enough." So, there I was again—too Black for the Mexicans, too Mexican for the Blacks.

I was becoming a man made of contradictions.

Even at school, the lessons on race made me feel invisible. When we learned about slavery, all eyes would slowly drift toward me—as if I was a living artifact. When we learned about Cesar Chavez and farmworkers, they looked toward each other. But never once did anyone, teacher or classmate, look at me as both. **It was like my very existence confused the curriculum.**

I began to internalize all of it. I started to believe I was less lovable. That I was meant to be angry. Meant to be violent. I started to see my own reflection as something to avoid. I envied the *light*. And worse, I began to resent my *dark*.

That's how colorism works. It doesn't need to be taught—it's absorbed. It's in the commercials, the novelas, the movies, the magazines. You're shown the hierarchy a thousand ways a day. And no matter how proud your Abuelita is, no matter how loving her arms may be, she can't always protect you from the daily messages that say: ***you're less because you're darker.***

My mother didn't help. If anything, she cemented the shame. She used "nigger" as if it were a punctuation mark. She made it clear that being Black was a disappointment, something to be hidden or fixed.

My mother loved her family. She loved her culture. But she hated the piece of me that didn't match it. And that hatred became my compass for how I viewed myself.

I remember one summer; I spent a week trying to lighten my skin. I stayed out of the sun, used bleach on my washcloth in the shower, like I could scrub off the "too much" from my DNA. I was nine.

Nine years old, and I already believed that my skin was a problem.

If you've never hated your own reflection, you may not understand how lonely that kind of childhood is. **It's like being in a family where everyone speaks a language you were born to understand but never invited to use.** And worse, you begin to wonder if love is something earned only through transformation.

So, I tried. I wore my clothes differently. Tried to style my hair like the "pretty boys" at church. I mimicked accents, downplayed my Blackness when around Mexicans and my Mexican-ness when around Black kids. I became a shape-shifter, mastering the art of blending in but never belonging.

But no amount of camouflage could protect me from colorism's bite. The deeper truth? Colorism isn't just prejudice—it's inheritance. My mother's shame wasn't born in her; it was passed to her. Somewhere in our family line, someone was told that whiter was safer. That lighter was smarter. That proximity to whiteness equaled validation. And she believed it enough to burn it into me.

Still, even in the face of all this pain, I held onto one truth: if colorism could be taught, it could be unlearned. I didn't have that language as a child, but I had the feeling. I had Abuelita. I had moments of pure love that weren't conditional on shade. And I began to see that this world—**this system that pits us against each other based on melanin—wasn't something natural. It was something constructed.**

And anything constructed can be destroyed.

But I wasn't ready to fight it yet. I was still drowning in the middle of it, letting it shape the way I viewed myself and others. I still found myself envying the lighter-skinned boys, still resenting the girls who looked through me like I was invisible.

I was lost, aching, and angry.

What I didn't realize then, but would come to understand later, is that my pain was political. My shame was systemic. And my hope—despite everything—was revolutionary.

Chapter 3:

When Home Feels Like Hostile Ground

They say home is where the heart is. But what happens when home becomes the first battlefield you ever know? When the people who are supposed to protect you end up teaching you pain in its most raw and intimate form?

For me, home wasn't safe. It was a place of emotional landmines—each room hiding something sharp, explosive, unpredictable. There was no warning system. No shelter. Just walls echoing with insults, screams, and the rhythm of belt leather slapping against skin.

My mother—who should've been my sanctuary—was often the sharpest edge in the house. Her words could kill softly and swiftly, and when they didn't, her hands followed. She wore her bitterness like armor and used her rage as a weapon. Sometimes, I think she hated the part of me that reminded her of the man who left. Other times, **I think she just hated herself and I was the mirror that refused to look away.**

Then there was Sid. My little brother's father. A man who should've never been trusted with children. Sid didn't just beat me—he tortured me. He stubbed cigarettes out on my shins like I was disposable. He waterboarded me in the bathtub, dunking me under water until my body spasmed from lack of air. He jammed thumbtacks into my back like I was a piece of paper on a corkboard.

And all of this happened while my mother "went to school." She knew, on some level, what was happening. I'd cry, beg her not to leave. But she always did. Maybe she was blind to it. Maybe she was just too ashamed to look. Either way, every time that front door closed behind her, I felt like a prisoner being left in the hands of a madman...

And I learned early how to scream without making a sound.

After Sid, came Rock—my little sister's father. A decorated Vietnam vet, a walking time bomb and Sid's brother. Rock was a Green Beret by title, but in our home, he was a tyrant. **He didn't beat me out of discipline. He beat me out of disgust.** My presence offended him. My skin was a constant reminder that I was not his. He'd spit words at me like "boy," "faggot," and "pussy" as if trying to strip me of any identity or confidence I might cling to.

He called me stupid and worthless so often, I started to believe it. No matter how I stood, how I spoke, how hard I tried—I was never enough for Rock.

Not Mexican enough...

Not male enough...

Not white enough...

Just "nigger" enough to hate.

Sometimes his flashbacks from the war would consume him. I remember one night waking up to my mother screaming. Rock was trying to throw her off the second-story balcony, shouting in Vietnamese. My brother and I stood there, paralyzed, unsure if this was a dream or just another Thursday night in our home.

It got worse. There was a day he chased us with a machete. Yes, a machete. My brother and I locked ourselves in the bathroom, standing on the toilet and sink while he slashed at our feet from under the door. That wasn't war. That was home.

But even when the trauma wasn't explosive, it was steady... daily... like a heartbeat that thumped pain instead of life. One of the worst beatings I ever got came after I flushed my report card down the toilet in the bathroom at school. I was terrified to bring home another report full of D's and F's. Rock found out and dragged me to the school. When I couldn't find the card, he threw me into a dumpster, bloodied my face, made me wade through old food and garbage, then threw me out like trash. Literally. A dark-skinned, bruised boy vomiting from the smell of rot, lying in his own filth and shame.

That was my home. That's what "discipline" looked like.

Afterward, he beat me again in my room so badly, I lost control of my body. I bled. I defecated. I passed out. When I came to, I was ordered to clean it all up like I was a slave. My mother? She threw a sponge at me and set down a bucket. Not a word of compassion. Not a moment of care.

How does a child grow up with love when his own body becomes a crime scene?

I remember the first time I thought seriously about killing them. I was in my early teens. My mother slapped me with her bra for drying it the wrong way. That slap—so small, so stupid—snapped something in me. I walked into the garage, found the butcher knife, and slipped it into my waistband.

I sat in my room with the knife next to me, waiting. Waiting for the belt. Waiting for the screams. Waiting for Rock's hand on my neck that would give me the excuse to end it all. But he never touched me again after that day.

I don't know if he saw the knife. I don't know if he just saw something different in my eyes. But something shifted. Maybe he sensed that the boy he used to beat into silence had finally reached a place beyond fear.

I never used the knife. But the decision to pick it up changed me. **It was the moment I stopped being a victim and started becoming something else—still broken, still hurting, but no longer defenseless.**

Years later, I'd begin to see that every abuser in that house was broken, too.

My mother? Broken by abandonment, shame, and self-hatred.

Sid? Who knows who broke him.

Rock? Probably still haunted by jungle ghosts and blood-stained medals. **But as a child, you don't have the language for generational trauma. You just know you're bleeding.**

What I didn't realize then is how trauma doesn't just shape how you survive—it shapes how you love, how you parent, how you treat yourself. I carried those bruises into my marriage. Into my fatherhood. Into every argument and insecurity. I became a man made from war zones.

And still, somehow, a small part of me believed that love was possible.

That's the paradox of trauma—you can be crushed by it but still cling to the dream of something gentler.

That dream kept me alive. That, and the memory of my Abuelita's arms—the only place where home ever felt like home.

Chapter 4:
Pretty Boy and the Broken Mirror

When you're born into two cultures but accepted by neither, you start looking for mirrors— people, places, ideas—that reflect something recognizable. **But sometimes, those mirrors show you only what you're not.**

For me, one of those mirrors was a kid at church I called "Pretty Boy."

He was everything I wasn't: light-skinned, clean-cut, always dressed in brand-new clothes, and glowing with privilege. His parents were always present, always smiling, always proud. He had a perfect smile, slick hair combed back like he stepped out of a novela, and a kind of unearned confidence that only comes when the world tells you you're special.

And then there was me.

The only Black kid in our catechism class. The one with dark skin, an afro, and invisible parents. The one who always sat alone at lunch. The one no one wanted to hold hands with during prayer. The one they whispered about, the one they called *mayate* under their breath—or sometimes out loud.

Pretty Boy never said much to me directly. He didn't have to. His smirk said it all. That tight-lipped, half-smile that kids learn from adults—a look soaked in judgment, superiority, and silent violence. It said, "You don't belong here. This is my world."

And the thing is… he was right.

Even in church—a place that preached love and brotherhood—I was an outcast. I didn't feel God's presence when we bowed our heads; I felt shame. I didn't find comfort in holy water or hymns. I found a hierarchy. I saw how Mexican kids circled around Pretty Boy like satellites orbiting the sun, basking in his approval, mimicking his disdain for me.

He was the mirror. And what I saw in him made me hate myself.

I'd like to tell you I took the high road. That I prayed for strength. That I talked to my grandmother about how I felt and that she calmed my spirit. But that's not what happened...

I stabbed him.

It was a Wednesday evening at catechism. We were lining up in the hallway before class when Pretty Boy floated past me with his little entourage. As usual, he gave me that look—smug and dismissive. But that day, something snapped.

We walked into the classroom single file. I waited, churning in violence. My fists clenched. My breathing shallow. Everything around me faded until all I could see was him. I grabbed a sharpened number two pencil from the teacher's desk and walked up behind him.

No one saw me.

I stabbed him low in the back, near his hip. I felt the pencil snap as it punctured his skin. He screamed and dropped. I tossed the broken pencil in the trash and walked away.

He was rushed to the hospital. I was never officially caught. No witnesses. But everyone suspected. Especially my Abuelita.

When the school called her in, I sat in the chair with my head down. She walked in, her face a mixture of sorrow and strength. She didn't ask me what happened. She didn't scold me or demand answers. She lifted my chin, looked me in the eyes, and said, *"Ay, mijo..."* before wrapping me in her arms.

That hug meant more to me than any confession or punishment. Because she *knew*. Not just what I'd done—but *why*.

She understood what it meant to be hated for your skin. She knew what it was to carry trauma silently, **to be cut a thousand times by words and stares and always be expected to bleed quietly.** She knew I had reached my breaking point.

Pretty Boy never came back to catechism class.

For a long time, I wrestled with guilt. Not only for hurting him physically—but for letting rage dictate who I was. I hated how easy it was to become what they already believed about me: violent, dangerous, angry. I played into the stereotype, and it haunted me.

But it also forced me to ask hard questions. Why did that one smirk break me? Why did I need him to acknowledge me, to see me? Why did I let a kid with good hair and fancy clothes define my worth?

Because that's what colorism does. It creates internal enemies. It makes you crave the approval of the very people who reject you. It makes you punish yourself—and sometimes others—for being born outside the box.

Looking back now, I realize Pretty Boy wasn't the enemy. He was a product. A child of a system that taught him to value light over dark. I don't know what became of him, but I hope he learned. I hope he grew out of that arrogance and into empathy. I hope we both did.

What I do know is this: **when you've been "othered" your whole life, violence becomes a language. And once you speak it, it takes years to learn a new one.**

That stabbing didn't solve anything. It didn't make me feel more accepted. If anything, it made me feel emptier. Like I'd given away a piece of myself just to be seen—even as a monster.

But that was the beginning of something. A slow unraveling. A questioning of what I wanted to become. I didn't have the answers yet. But I was starting to understand the stakes.

This world would never stop trying to define me. But maybe, just maybe, I could start defining myself.

Chapter 5:

My Mother, the Mirror, and Her Lies

If my Abuelita was my safe place, then my mother was the battlefield I couldn't escape. She was both the reason I lived and the reason I wanted to die. For most kids, a mother's love is oxygen. For me, it was fire—hot, unpredictable, and always threatening to burn me alive.

My mother was Mexican-American, born and raised in Fresno, California. To outsiders, she was a hardworking woman—attending college, raising three kids, and holding down her household. But behind closed doors, she was something else entirely. Cold. Violent. Bitter. And deeply ashamed of me.

From as early as I can remember, I understood something about myself was "wrong" in her eyes. It wasn't the way I talked or the way I walked. It wasn't even my behavior—though I gave her plenty of reasons to be upset. No, it was my skin. My Blackness.

When we'd walk through the neighborhood and pass a Black man, she'd spit venom under her breath: "Look at that sorry-ass nigger." If it was a Black woman: "Filthy ass bitch." My little brother and I would laugh—not because we understood, but because we were children and the word "nigger" sounded like one of the bad words we weren't supposed to say. Cursing felt grown, and so we giggled in ignorance.

But by fifth grade, I stopped laughing. Because by then, I understood what the word meant...and I understood what she meant when she used it on me.

It wasn't just hate. It was rejection.

She would compare me to my light-skinned cousins, the ones with light eyes and silky hair. They got her affection, her approval. I got her contempt. She'd look at me and see a mistake—a permanent reminder of the Black man who fathered me and vanished.

She never said his name. Never showed me a picture. All I knew was that he was a "pimp" and once brought his "hoes" to the hospital to see me after I was born. That was it. That was the entirety of my paternal legacy. **I didn't have a dad—I had a stain.**

And so, my mother projected all her pain onto me.

She hit me, screamed at me, called me names. She mocked my hair, my nose, my lips. She humiliated me for struggling in school, beat me for gagging on food she knew I hated. One time, she slammed my face into the kitchen table after I vomited butter drenched green beans onto my plate. My nose bled into the food. She didn't care. She screamed at me to clean myself up—and then made me eat what was left.

I was maybe seven.

That was the moment I stopped seeing her as a mother and started seeing her as my oppressor.

After that, the dynamic shifted. I no longer sought her approval. I no longer feared her, even though I still hurt from her. I started to recognize that she wasn't just broken—she was shattering me on purpose. And for what? Because I reminded her of the man who left? Because I didn't come out light enough to pass?

I began to understand that her hatred for me wasn't born the day I misbehaved. It was inherited. Conditioned. Cultivated over generations.

Somewhere along the way, she'd learned to believe that Blackness was filth. That it was failure. And when I was born, carrying the features of a father she loathed and a culture she feared, she couldn't love me without confronting herself.

So, she never did.

Her self-hate became my identity. Her lies became my mirror.

But I wasn't the only one she lied to. She cheated on Sid. Then cheated on Rock. And to make things worse, she cheated on Sid *with* Rock—who happened to be Sid's brother. Which means my little brother and little sister are cousins.

When I found that out, it wasn't even shocking. It was just more of the same: chaos, secrets, twisted definitions of love and family. She'd shrug it off and say, "At least I kept it in the family." Like that made it better.

Her lies weren't limited to who she slept with. She lied about where we went, who we saw. I remember her dragging us to a man named Jessie's house for "visits." We'd sit in the living room with his daughter, watching T.V while they disappeared into the back. My mother would tell us afterward, "If your dad asks where we were, say we were with Grandma."

I stopped trusting anything she said. Every smile she gave me felt like a setup. Every apology was just a commercial break before the next episode of abuse...

And yet, even with all that, I still wanted her to love me.

That's the cruelest part of it all—**children don't stop loving the parent who breaks them. They just learn to love themselves less in the process.**

It took years before I could look at her and see the full truth. That she, too, was a product of trauma. That she didn't come out of the womb this hateful. She was made. Molded by her own history, her own disappointments. Somewhere inside her, there was probably a little girl who just wanted to be held and wasn't. But knowing that doesn't excuse how she treated me.

Understanding someone's pain doesn't mean you let them keep inflicting it.

Eventually, I would have to stop looking at her for answers. She couldn't give me what she didn't have. She couldn't show me love when she never learned how to receive it herself.

So, I stopped chasing her approval. I stopped trying to be the son she could brag about. I started trying to be the man I needed when I was seven years old, curled up in the corner, praying to a God I barely believed in.

Chapter 6:
No Man's Son

I never met my father...

Let me rephrase that—I never *knew* my father. I was told his name was Joe, and that he was a "pimp." That's what my mother said with the kind of disgust that stuck to my skin like oil. The only story she shared was that he brought two of his prostitutes to the hospital after I was born, "to show off his baby." That was the end of the fairy tale. No bedtime stories, no "he held you once and cried," no "he was proud of you." Just a ghost, dressed in gold rings and shame.

I didn't even see a picture of him until I was nearly 40. One of my uncles on his side showed it to me when I tracked down that part of my bloodline in 2011. Until that moment, I lived my entire childhood, adolescence, and much of my adulthood staring at a mirror without a blueprint. I'd look at my dark skin, my lips, my nose and wonder where those pieces came from. And more hauntingly, *why* he left.

A boy needs a father. Not just for guidance or discipline, but to show him what being a man looks like. To show him how to navigate the world in his own body. To show him that he is *seen*.

I never got that.

Instead, I got secondhand stories. Whispers. Assumptions. My mother painted him as worthless, a user, a nobody. But even when she cursed him, I leaned in. I wanted *anything*. Even her hate gave me a sliver of connection to the man who made me.

As I grew up in a house full of beatings, insults, and locked doors, I started to imagine what my life would've been like if he'd stayed. Would I have walked taller?

Would I have understood how to move through the world as a Black boy instead of being abused by people who hated that part of me? Would I have known how to *be* Black?

Because that's another layer to this. It's not just about missing a father. It's about missing Black identity. I was being raised in a full Mexican environment, and while I appreciate my culture deeply, it came with one glaring issue—I wasn't allowed to be Black. At least not proudly. Not openly.

There were no Black cookouts. No blues on Sunday mornings. No stories about Malcolm, Martin, or Mandela. I didn't learn about the Tuskegee Airmen or Marcus Garvey. There were no affirmations of my hair, my skin, my voice. There was no *history* that looked like me.

Instead, I got the Mexican version of "Black": the "chango" jokes, the warnings not to act "too Black," the constant reminders that I was *different*, even within my own family. I was the one who needed extra discipline. The one who needed to stay out of the sun. The one whose existence was proof that my mother made a mistake.

But in school, I wasn't Mexican enough either. The few Black kids I met said I "talked white" or "acted Mexican." I didn't have rhythm. I didn't know the music. I had no swag, no cultural language. I was a cultural orphan.

So, I started searching for masculinity wherever I could find it—on TV, in rap lyrics, in the streets. Black men I watched on Soul Train, Yo MTV Raps and Amateur Night at The Apollo became my reference points. I mimicked their confidence, their moves, their coolness. But it was an act. I was just trying to fill the void. Trying to be *somebody's* son.

By ninth grade, the absence became unbearable. That was when I first seriously tried to end my life. I stuck my head in the oven and inhaled deeply. I wanted it to end. Not because I hated life, but because I couldn't find a reason to keep going. **I felt invisible. And when you're invisible long enough, death starts to look like clarity.**

I didn't die that day. God pulled me back— But the damage was done. Not just the attempt, but the realization: I had to raise myself.

I had to become my own father.

That's what's cruel about fatherlessness—it makes you grow up too fast. It teaches you to pretend you're whole when you're splintered. I had to guess what it meant to be a man, to love a woman, to express pain without rage. I stumbled through it, bruised people along the way, and wore my trauma like armor.

Years later, I would stare at him in an old photograph. He looked like me. That was both healing and haunting. Because if he looked like me, then maybe he hurt like me, too. **Maybe he didn't leave because he didn't care. Maybe he left because he didn't know how to stay.**

Maybe he was just as broken as the rest of us.

I still wonder what he would've said if we met. Would he apologize? Would he make excuses? Would he cry? Or would he lie, the way people do when they don't want to admit their absence caused a lifetime of damage?

I don't know. I will never know.

But I've made peace with one thing—I am not his ghost. I am not the mistake he ran from. I am not the absence he left behind.

I am my own man now.

Chapter 7:
MY PEOPLE
TURNED ON ME

I t's a strange thing when the people who look like you, suddenly look at you like a stranger.

Growing up in Fresno during the 1980s, gang culture wasn't just background noise—it was the beat of the streets. It filled our music, our clothing, our language, our bodies. After the movie *Colors* dropped—starring Bloods and Crips locked in a deadly rivalry—everything around me changed. It was like someone flipped a switch, and my city went from neighborhood pride to tribal war.

Before that summer, I had a few "friends"—mostly Mexican-American boys from my elementary school, middle school and neighborhood. We were cool. We ditched class together, fought side by side, when necessary, shared snacks and secrets. We were all troubled, angry, looking for somewhere to belong. And for a while, we belonged to each other.

But when the movie dropped, and the soundtrack hit the streets—especially Ice-T's title track—it was like gasoline got poured on dry wood. "Colors... Colors..." That beat didn't just bang—it bled.

When we came back to school after summer, the line had been drawn. And it wasn't just red and blue—it was Brown and Black.

Suddenly, the Mexican boys were wearing red, calling themselves Bloods. And the Black boys were throwing blue, claiming Crip. And there I was—stuck in the middle. Half-

Black. Half-Mexican. No color to claim. No gang to call mine.

That first day back, I walked up to one of my closest friends—one I'd known since elementary. I tapped him on the shoulder, ready to joke about the break, maybe ask what he did over summer.

He turned around, eyes cold, jaw tight. "Fuck you, cuzz," he spat, shoving me hard in the chest. "This Blood over here."

I laughed at first, thinking it was a joke. But then another guy shoved me from behind. "What's up, cuzz?" he growled, dropping into the classic Chicano pre-fight stance. One leg forward, fists up, face twisted in rage.

I barely had time to react. My body took over before my brain did. I spun around and cracked him with a right hook so hard he dropped like a sack of concrete. The smack of his head hitting the floor echoed through the hallway.

As he crumpled, my former friend lunged at me, yelling, "Motherfuckin nigger!"

That word. That firebrand word, thrown in my face by someone who shared my skin tone, my block, my childhood. It unlocked something in me.

I landed a left cross that shattered his nose, followed by a right that split his lip. Blood flew. Screams followed. Teachers rushed in.

The next thing I knew, we were all in the principal's office. His parents came storming in, cursing me out in Spanish: "Pinche mayate!" "Sucio negrito!" They didn't know—or maybe they didn't care—that I spoke Spanish too. I understood every insult. Every syllable pierced my skin like glass.

But then my Abuelita walked in...

And everything stopped.

She didn't look scared or ashamed. She looked like a lioness protecting her cub. She saw me bruised but standing. And when those parents sneered at her, asking if that "mayate" was her son, she didn't blink.

"Sí, cabrón," she said, standing taller. "¿Y cómo que mayate? ¿Te has mirado en un espejo? ¡Tu culo es más negro que el suyo!"

Translation? *"Yes, asshole, he's my son. And what do you mean, 'nigger'? Have you looked in a mirror? Your ass is darker than his!"*

They didn't know what to say. Shame crept into their faces. One mother even apologized. But I wasn't looking at them. I was staring at my grandmother, my hero. **She didn't just defend me. She *declared* me.**

That moment reminded me that I wasn't crazy. That the line between love and hate wasn't about color—it was about ignorance. Fear. Insecurity. And power.

But even so, the damage was done. That day made it clear: to some people, blood doesn't matter. Shared culture doesn't matter. Childhood bonds don't matter.

All that mattered was the color you were willing to kill or die for.

And for me, I was colorless. Crip kids didn't trust me because I spoke Spanish and ate chorizo at home. Bloods didn't trust me because I had Black skin. I was a ghost in both camps. A liability. A puzzle they didn't want to solve.

So, I kept fighting.

I fought for respect. I fought to prove I wasn't weak. I fought because if I didn't, I'd disappear. That's what survival looked like back then. Every punch I threw felt like shouting, *I exist! I belong!*

But inside, I didn't feel tough. I felt tired. Confused. Betrayed.

Because these weren't strangers calling me "nigger." These were my people. My mother. My classmates. My neighbors. People whose skin matched mine, who came from the same streets, the same struggles.

But they didn't see me as one of them. Not anymore.

That's the curse of being bi-racial in a divided world. You're constantly asked to choose sides. But when you don't fit neatly into a box, both sides will often reject you.

What they didn't realize—and what I hadn't learned yet—is that I *wasn't* half this and half that.

I was *both*.

Fully Black. Fully Mexican. And fully fed up with trying to shrink myself to make others comfortable.

That lesson would take years to own. But that hallway? That punch? That word "nigger" from a friend?

It was the beginning.

The moment I stopped trying to be accepted…

And started trying to be whole.

Chapter 8:
BACK TO SCHOOL, BACK TO SHAME

For most kids, school is a second home—a place where you can learn, grow, explore, and maybe even escape the chaos at home. But for me, school was just another front in the war for belonging.

The classroom was never a safe haven. It was another spotlight on everything I lacked: patience, focus, support... and most painfully, acceptance. I didn't walk through those hallways with the quiet confidence of a kid who knew he mattered. I walked in with the weight of being "too Black" for the Mexican kids and "too Mexican" for the Black ones. An outsider in every homeroom.

Teachers didn't know what to do with me. I had trouble reading, struggled to write, and couldn't sit still. Homework confused me. Directions felt like foreign languages. But what I lacked in comprehension, I made up for in survival instincts. I knew how to fake it. How to laugh when I didn't get the joke. How to pretend I was failing on purpose just so they wouldn't think I was stupid.

Because nothing stings like feeling *dumb*. Nothing.

And it wasn't just the academic failure. It was the public shame that came with it. Like when the teacher passed back tests face-up, and I'd see nothing but red pen and the letter "F" scrawled at the top. Or when we had to read aloud and my mouth dried up because I didn't want to trip over the words and become the joke of the day. The kids would laugh. Sometimes the teacher would sigh like I was wasting everyone's time.

One time, I turned in a math worksheet where all the answers were wrong. I knew it when I handed it over. But I didn't know how to ask for help. When I got it back, the teacher called me to the front of the class and said loud enough for everyone to hear, "Maybe you should focus on learning English before you try to learn math."

I remember everyone laughing. Some kids looked confused. Others just stared at me, waiting to see how I'd react. I did what I always did—laughed it off like it didn't hurt. But inside, I wanted to disappear. Crawl under a desk and vanish. Maybe forever.

The irony? English *was* my language. But that didn't matter. Because to her, my skin told a different story. A story of failure. Of unworthiness. Of inferiority.

That's how institutional racism works—it doesn't always yell. Sometimes it just whispers, *"you're not meant to succeed here."*

But it wasn't just the teachers. It was the other kids too. Mexican kids who looked like me but didn't claim me. Black kids who called me a "white boy" and mocked my non-slang, non-Ebonics lingo. I once had a group of Mexican girls sitting behind me call me "negro feo"—ugly Black boy—every day during lunch. They said it softly, behind giggles, like it was a game.

And I just sat there, clenching my tray, my fists, my jaw.

Every insult became another crack in the dam that was holding back the ocean inside me.

Eventually, I stopped trying. What was the point? When you're convinced that no one sees your potential, why even look for it yourself?

So, I started skipping class. Hanging out behind buildings, robbing, stealing, cussing, vandalizing. I started fights just to feel something. I'd beat up kids I didn't even hate. Not for the respect. For the power. For the control. Because school taught me early on: *if you can't win, at least don't be weak.*

My grades tanked. I got detention constantly. Suspensions became routine. Each phone call home came with fresh bruises—courtesy of my mother or Rock, depending on who was angriest. It was a vicious cycle: act out, get punished, act out worse, get punished harder.

No teachers asked me why I was angry. Why I was failing. Why I couldn't sit still. No one knew about the beatings, the sleepless nights, the hunger, the suicidal thoughts, or the trauma I carried like a backpack filled with bricks.

They didn't want to know.

But the truth is, I wasn't stupid. I wasn't lazy. I wasn't just "bad."

I was traumatized.

I was a child trying to learn in a system that didn't understand boys like me. A system not built for complexity, especially not the kind that comes in dark skin with bilingual trauma.

And yet—somehow—I survived it. Not with straight A's or valedictorian speeches. But with scraps of dignity. With a growing awareness that the problem wasn't just me—it was the world I was forced to navigate.

Later in life, I'd meet Black and Brown kids who'd tell me the same thing: "School never felt safe." "I thought I was dumb." "They just gave up on me."

And I'd realize, I wasn't alone.

But back then, in those crowded hallways and silent classrooms, it sure felt like I was.

Still, even in all the shame, a seed was planted. A small, stubborn belief that maybe—just maybe—I could write my own story someday. That my identity wasn't a burden, but a blueprint.

And that the world's inability to teach me didn't mean I couldn't learn.

Chapter 9:

BURNED BY THE BELT, SAVED BY THE CORNER

D iscipline, they called it.

That's how they justified the beatings. That's how my mother and Rock explained away the bruises, the blood, the hours of isolation. It wasn't abuse—it was discipline. Correction. Tough love. But I can tell you firsthand: there was nothing loving about it.

A belt has a sound you never forget. Before it strikes your body, it cuts through the air with a whistle, slicing silence in half. Then comes the sting, the burn, the shock. Followed by a pause—just long enough for fear to set in—before the next one lands. Again, and again. Until the welts rise. Until your screams blend into whimpers. Until you stop fighting and just take it.

I learned to go numb. I had to.

Rock was the master of punishment. His weapon of choice was a thick, black leather belt—the kind you'd see on a biker or in a military barracks. He used it like a sword, like it was forged to teach black boys like me a lesson I'd never forget... And I didn't.

Once, after lying about a report card I'd flushed down the toilet, he dragged me from our apartment to the school, made me dig through trash cans, and finally threw me into a dumpster when I couldn't find it. That was just the warm-up.

Later that night, I stood in my room, pants around my ankles, bare skin trembling. Rock slammed the door behind him, belt in hand, eyes blazing. When I didn't turn around fast enough, he lashed the belt across the front of my legs, hitting my private parts in the process. I screamed. I covered myself. He kept swinging. When I fell, he lifted me by my shirt, slammed me into the wall, and beat me until I passed out.

I woke up in a puddle of urine, blood, and feces. The room smelled like fear and failure. Poop had splattered the walls. My body shook with every breath. And still, my mother didn't ask if I was okay. She brought a bucket, threw a sponge at my feet, and said, "Take off your clothes, throw them in the trash and clean this shit up."

So, I crawled. Naked. Broken. Cleaning my blood and shame off the floor like it was normal.

That was discipline.

But here's the twist—the beatings eventually stopped.

It happened after I snapped in the garage. I was about fifteen. My mother slapped me with her bra for drying it in the machine. I clenched my fists. I stood over her, breathing heavy. Her voice dripped with venom as she dared me to hit her, called me a "sorry-ass nigger like your father." And for the first time, I didn't flinch. I didn't back down.

I didn't hit her—but I thought about it.

That night, I sat in my room with a butcher knife resting on the floor beside my bed, blade up, handle tilted toward me. I didn't sleep. I waited for Rock to come in with that belt. I waited to kill him...

But he only told me to go to bed.

And he never laid a hand on me again.

From that day on, the punishments changed. No more belts. No more fists. Just silence. Isolation. Psychological warfare.

They made me stand in the corner. Sometimes for five, six, seven months straight. No birthday parties. No holidays. No dinner. Just a patch of wall, a hard floor, and the weight of my own thoughts.

I'd come home from school and walk straight to the corner. No talking. No eye contact. Just silence. I'd stand there from 3:00pm to bedtime at 10:00pm. No food. No water. No bathroom breaks unless I begged.

But I wasn't completely alone.

My little brother would sneak food from his plate, stuff it into his mouth, then walk over and spit it into my palm when no one was looking. I'd do the same for him when it was his turn. We survived like prisoners in the same cell, passing crumbs and compassion in secret.

At the time, I hated the corner. I hated the hunger, the aching feet, the boredom. But looking back, the corner saved me in a way the beatings never could.

It gave me silence... Stillness... A place to think.

It became a meditation room, even if I didn't know that's what it was. I replayed memories, mapped out fantasies, dreamed of escape. I learned how to live inside my mind. I didn't have a therapist. I didn't have language for "trauma" or "emotional regulation." But I had those hours. Those months. Those years. Those endless, quiet moments where no one could hit me, yell at me, or look at me with disgust.

I found myself there.

Not fully. Not peacefully. But just enough to hold on.

That's what trauma does—it makes you resourceful. It forces you to find cracks of light in rooms with no windows. And somehow, even in the corner, I learned to imagine more. To want more. To believe that life didn't have to be this way forever.

That's the strange legacy of abuse—it doesn't always end with the final blow. Sometimes it echoes into generations. But sometimes, if you're lucky, it ends with a promise.

And I made mine, facing the wall, tears dry, stomach empty—but spirit intact.

Chapter 10:
TRYING TO DIE TO UNDERSTAND LIFE

I was thirteen the first time I tried to kill myself.

The attempt wasn't elegant, dramatic, or even well-thought-out. It wasn't a cry for help. It was a surrender. A slow collapse beneath the weight of shame, beatings, and a silence that screamed louder than anything I could ever say.

It happened on a Saturday. My mom and Rock were arguing again—something about a bill, or maybe someone cheating. Their voices weren't new. They were part of the soundtrack of my life. Doors slammed. Vulgar language. Fists pounded into walls. I sat in the corner, not as punishment that day, but out of instinct. It was the safest place to be: out of sight, out of mind.

I hadn't eaten much. My stomach twisted with hunger and fear, two feelings I had learned to ignore. I stood up slowly, my feet aching from hours of standing. I wandered into the kitchen and stared at the oven like it was calling me. It was old—white with black knobs, the pilot light always struggling to stay lit.

I released the gas, I opened it, knelt, and stuck my head inside.

No note. No tears. No last prayer.

Just exhaustion.

By thirteen, I had already been locked in closets, beaten with belts, humiliated in front of teachers, stabbed a kid in catechism, and been told by my own mother that I would never be anything more than a sorry-ass nigger like the father I never met.

At thirteen, I already knew I wasn't wanted.

I wasn't scared to die. I was scared to *keep living like this*.

But God intervened. The gas didn't kill me. Maybe the oven was too old, too broken to finish what I'd started. Maybe I was, too.

I collapsed on the floor, not crying, barely breathing. Just *alive*.

That moment didn't save me. It didn't wake me up or teach me to be grateful for life. It didn't heal anything. It simply paused my death long enough for something else to unfold later.

That's what people don't understand about suicidal thoughts—**sometimes, it's not about wanting to die. It's about not knowing how to live with the weight of what's died inside you.**

It wasn't my last attempt either. Later in life, I swallowed a handful of pills, washing them down with alcohol. Another time, I walked onto train tracks and dared myself to stay put. But something always pulled me back.

Anger... A flicker of hope...God... The memory of Abuelita's arms... I don't know. I just know I kept waking up. Kept breathing.

But each attempt left a scar—an invisible one. A reminder that I had stood at the edge and looked into the void and whispered, *maybe.*

Sometimes, I wonder what my mother would've done if I'd succeeded. Would she have cried? Blamed herself? Denied everything? Would Rock have even noticed? Would my little brother and sister grow up wondering where I went?

Or would they have just replaced me with silence?

I'll never know. And maybe that's for the best.

What I do know is that every time I stood on the edge, I was just looking for a reason *not to* jump. I was searching for proof that life could be more than pain. That there was something on the other side of this storm worth surviving for.

And the truth is—I started to find it.

Not all at once. Not in a single moment. But piece by piece.

I found it in the rhythm, in the poetry of rap music. I found it in basketball courts and breakdancing sessions. I found it in the eyes of girls who saw past my anger and into my loneliness. I found it in books, in writing, in therapy—years later, yes, but eventually.

And most of all, I found it in the decision to live *for something,* even when I didn't yet know what that something was.

At first, that "something" was survival. Then it became love. Then my wife. Then healing. And now? Now it's purpose.

To tell the truth...

To break the silence...

To become the man I never saw, the example I never knew.

And to remind kids like me—those stuck in homes where love wears a mask of violence—that they are not broken. They are not invisible. They are not crazy for wanting the pain to stop.

They are survivors.

Even if survival, at times, feels like slow drowning.

Even if some days the best you can do is breathe.

That counts...

That matters...

I don't glamorize my past. I don't wear my scars like medals. But I honor them. Because they remind me that **I tried to die not because I was weak—but because no one had ever shown me how strong I already was.**

So now I live. Loudly. Fully. Messy.

Because every breath I take is a rebellion against the silence that almost killed me.

Chapter 11:

THE BURDEN OF
BEING BLACK IN
BROWN SPACES

I was always Black in the wrong places.

In my own home. In school. In church. At family gatherings. At the corner store. Every room I stepped into with my extended family (by marriage) reminded me that I was wearing skin that didn't match the rest of the photograph.

Not that anyone said it directly—at least not always. But the looks were enough. The silence. The shift in energy when I entered a room. The way the light-skinned cousins got pulled in for hugs while I was asked to help carry chairs or clean something up. The way people would lower their voices when talking about "Moreno" people as if I wasn't sitting right there.

When I was little, I didn't understand what was happening. I just knew that when I showed up to a party, the vibe changed. That my mother laughed more when I wasn't around. That Abuelita's neighbors stared at me like I'd stolen something, even when I was just playing in the dirt. I thought maybe it was my clothes. Or the way I spoke. Or the way I sat. I thought if I smiled more, or helped more, I could make them see I belonged.

But the truth was, they didn't see me as one of them...

They saw me as *Black*.

And for many of them—maybe not out of malice, maybe just out of conditioning   that meant I was less.

I started hearing the term *pelo malo*—"bad hair." That's how they referred to my curls, my texture. My light-skinned cousins had "good hair"—soft, wavy, manageable. Mine was "difficult," "wild," "nappy." They'd joke about how I must've inherited it from "el chango"—the monkey. Laughing, always laughing.

But those laughs stayed with me.

So, I tried to fix myself. I'd put lotion in my hair to flatten it. Press it down with hats. Try to look more like them, even if it meant hiding myself.

That's what the burden felt like—this constant need to adjust, to shrink, to perform.

In school, I did the same thing. I sat with the Mexican kids because they spoke the language I grew up with. We shared snacks, TV shows, cuss words. But there was always that invisible line. I could laugh with them, but I wasn't *them*. Not really. Not when their older brothers called me *mayate*. Not when the girls said they didn't date dark-skinned guys. Not when the fights started and I had to choose a side that didn't exist for me.

I was too Black for the Brown kids...

And too Brown for the Black ones...

When I tried to hang with Black students, I was hit with "You talk white," or "You ain't really Black." They mocked my English, my cadence, my lack of Black "swag." I didn't know the songs they knew. I wasn't raised on collard greens or Sunday gospel. I didn't know how to brush waves or play spades. I couldn't even fake it.

I was a stranger in both homes.

There's a unique kind of exhaustion that comes from constantly code-switching between cultures you were born into but never truly accepted by. I had to juggle accents, slang, posture, tone, *even eye contact* depending on who I was around.

But no matter how much I tried to fit in—I didn't.

And that was the lie I'd been told: that if I just worked harder, I could earn my place.

But identity isn't something you earn.

It's something you claim.

It took me years to unlearn that.

Years of swallowing the casual anti-Blackness that lives in Brown communities. Years of hearing family members call dark-skinned people *feos*, *changos*. Years of seeing lightness treated as royalty and darkness as disease. Years of watching how Black features were mocked on us but praised when adopted by lighter-skinned people—when it became "trendy."

Even in relationships, the pattern repeated. Latina girls would say, "You're cute… for a Black guy." Some would date me in secret but never bring me around their friends. I was the taboo they were willing to taste—but not keep.

That's the burden. Not just existing between worlds—but existing beneath them.

You start to ask yourself dangerous questions:

What am I, if nobody wants all of me?

How much of myself do I have to lose just to be seen?

But even in the heaviest moments, I knew this wasn't my shame to carry.

I didn't create this division. I didn't invent the hierarchy that says light is right and Black is bad. That was taught. Fed. Recycled. Passed down like a family heirloom wrapped in silence.

Colorism is a colonial virus—planted by white supremacy and watered by self-hatred.

And for centuries, it's worked. It kept Black and Brown divided. It kept us so busy judging each other's shade that we forgot the enemy was the system telling us there's a "better" shade at all.

When I finally started to unpack all this—through reading, therapy, reflection—I realized I didn't have to choose a side.

I am *both*.

Fully Black. Fully Mexican.

Not a mistake. Not a mix-up. Not a problem to be solved.

A fusion. A bridge. A possibility.

That doesn't mean the burden disappeared. I still walk into rooms where people choose to only see half of me—or none of me at all. I still feel the sting when someone tries to explain my own identity to me.

But now I carry it differently.

Not with shame...

With fire...

Because if I'm going to be seen as a threat no matter where I go...

...I might as well be a threat *to the system that taught us to hate ourselves.*

Chapter 12:
ABUELITA, MY SAVIOR

I n every war, there's a sanctuary. A place where the noise quiets, the wounds begin to close, and you can finally breathe without looking over your shoulder.

For me, that sanctuary was my Abuelita.

Her name was Esperanza—Spanish for "hope"—and that's exactly what she was. While the rest of my world told me I was too dark, too angry, too much or not enough, **Abuelita looked at me and saw only love. She saw a grandson, not a problem. A child, not a burden.**

In her home, I wasn't the Black kid. I wasn't the mistake my mother regretted or the punching bag Rock beat down. I was *mijo*. Her "son." Even when I towered over her, even when my voice deepened, even when the world hardened me, I was still her baby.

She made me believe in softness, when everything else around me demanded steel.

I used to sit in her kitchen on Saturday mornings, legs swinging from a chair too tall for me, the smell of chorizo and homemade tortillas filling the air. She'd hum old rancheras and call me "gordito," even though I was all bones and bruises. She'd fix my plate like I was royalty—stacking my favorite food just the way I liked it.

And when I'd break down—when my silence turned to sobs she couldn't ignore—she'd pull me into her lap, wrap her short, strong arms around me, and whisper, *"No estás solo, mijo. Nunca estás solo."* You're not alone. Never alone.

Those words saved me more times than I can count.

She knew what was happening at home. Not all the details, not the extent of the abuse, not every bruise—but enough. Enough to hold me tighter. Enough to sneak me extra food when I wasn't allowed to eat. Enough to defend me against people who talked slick behind my back.

I remember one time at a family gathering, one of my aunts made a comment about "how dark Jaime was getting." She said it with a smirk, like I was something she was disappointed to see bloom in our family's flowerbed. Abuelita didn't miss a beat. She snapped, "And what, mija? You think light skin makes you better? Go look at your father's life and tell me what 'light' has done for him."

The room went quiet...

No one ever made a comment like that again when she was around.

She wasn't loud or confrontational by nature. But for me? She'd roar.

I don't think she ever fully understood how deeply her love cut through the shame I carried. When I hated my hair, she'd run her fingers through it like it was silk. When I sulked because the other kids called me "mayate," **she'd press her**

forehead to mine and remind me how beautiful my skin was. She told me I was handsome when no one else did. Smart when everyone else had written me off. Worthy when I felt like nothing.

She saw *me*—all of me. Not half this, half that. Not too dark or too loud or too broken.

Just *me*.

The older I got, the more I realized how radical that kind of love really is.

Because she had every reason to believe the lies the world taught about Blackness. She grew up in a system soaked in colorism, racism, and colonial legacy. She was surrounded by whispers that light was right, and dark was dangerous. She heard the same jokes, saw the same beauty standards, sat in the same churches that painted Jesus with blond hair, blue eyes and called people like me "pobrecitos."

But she chose *not* to pass that on.

She broke the cycle.

Maybe it was instinct. Maybe it was her own pain. Maybe it was wisdom that came from years of watching people suffer quietly.

Whatever it was, it made her different.

She never talked about her own childhood much, but I saw the scars in her eyes. The way she moved so carefully through family conversations. The way she kept photos but rarely smiled in them. The way she lit candles for people she never spoke of. **She knew suffering. But she didn't transfer it to me.**

She transformed it.

Her house, even when small and worn down, felt like a palace. Because in that house, I was whole. I didn't have to explain myself. I didn't have to defend my existence. I didn't have to choose between my Blackness and my Brownness.

I could just *be*.

That's why, even now, decades later, I measure every safe space I find by how close it feels to her presence.

When I meet someone who listens without judgment—*Abuelita*.

When I feel safe enough to cry without shame—*Abuelita*.

When I catch the scent of chorizo and masa in the air—*Abuelita*.

She once told me the world would know my name. She often told me I was *enough*. That I was loved. That I mattered.

And that was more powerful than any sermon, any lecture, any therapy session.

She didn't live to see the man I became, the award-winning author... **But she *made* him.** Every moment of compassion. Every plate of food. Every bedtime blessing. Every whispered prayer in the kitchen.

She gave me a name. Not Jaime the mistake. Not Jaime the bastard. Not Jaime the burden.

Jaime her mijo.

And when you've been through what I've been through, sometimes that's all you need to keep going.

Just one person who sees you. Who stays. Who saves you without even trying.

Esperanza was that person.

She was my savior...

My guardian angel...

My Abuelita.

Chapter 13:

FROM RAGE TO REDEMPTION

Rage was my first language. Before I ever understood love or empathy, I knew how to clench a fist. I knew how to break things. How to throw words like knives and how to destroy anything that reminded me of weakness—including myself.

Violence had always been the currency in my house. When my mother was angry, she screamed, slapped, spit and punched. When Rock was upset, he beat and humiliated. When extended family cousins picked on me, they used words, exclusion. I never saw a disagreement handled with grace. I never saw apologies delivered with vulnerability. **I learned early that rage was safer than sadness. And I carried that into adulthood like a badge of survival.**

So, when I met my wife, I didn't know how to love—I only knew how to control.

My relationship was shaped by the echoes of my own childhood. I yelled. I cheated. I manipulated. I played the tough guy. I didn't know how to listen without getting defensive, how to be present without dominating. I saw every request as a challenge, every argument as war.

And the woman I married paid the price.

I didn't just break her, I shattered her. Not all at once—but slowly, like rust spreading through a frame. I brought the blueprint of my own abuse into our home and passed it on like a curse I didn't know I carried. I was verbally abusive.

Emotionally violent. I cheated on her repeatedly and convinced myself it was normal— **"just a man being a man."**

I used my pain as an excuse, a crutch.

But one day, everything changed.

She looked at me with tears in her eyes—not from fear, not from anger, but from exhaustion. And she uttered a sentence I'll never forget:

"I love you not for the man you are, but for the man you will become."

That was the moment my mirror cracked.

It wasn't about her anymore. It was about me. My childhood. My mother's voice still echoing inside my head. Rock's belt still swinging in my mind. The trauma still living in my bones, directing my actions like a puppet master.

I had to choose.

Continue the cycle...

Or break it...

So... I broke.

I broke open. I cried in front of her for the first time. Not the angry tears that came from rage—but deep, guttural sobs that came from shame. I told her about Sid. About Rock. About my suicide attempts. About the green beans, the bathtub, the belt, the closet and the silence. I told her everything.

And then I did the thing that terrified me most...

I asked for help.

I started therapy. Real therapy. Not just venting to friends or journaling when I was mad—but sitting with professionals. Digging into childhood trauma. Naming emotions I never knew how to identify. Learning how to breathe through discomfort instead of exploding. Learning how to apologize without conditions. Learning how to love without possession.

It was like being reborn through pain.

There were setbacks. Moments when the old me tried to resurface. Times when I raised my voice and had to step away. Times when I almost lied but caught myself in the nick of time. But every small act of change was a revolution. A rebellion against the broken boy I once was.

And something incredible happened...

My wife began to heal too.

Her laughter came back. Her glow returned. The walls she'd built brick by brick around her heart started to lower. **We began to rediscover each other—not just as partners, but as people fighting to unlearn generational damage.**

She wasn't perfect. I wasn't either. But together, we made a choice: *We will learn how to love.*

That became our mission. To rewrite the narrative. To replace rage with reflection. To replace violence with vulnerability.

That's redemption.

Not perfection. Not erasing the past.

But choosing to build a future from the rubble.

My rage didn't disappear. It still lives inside me. **But now it has a seat, not a steering wheel.** I acknowledge it. I manage it. I don't let it make my choices.

Healing is not a straight line. It's a winding road full of dead ends and hidden paths. But every step away from the man I was is a victory.

I am no longer defined by the pain I inherited…

I am defined by the healing I *chose*.

Chapter 14:

Brown and Black: A Love Letter to Unity

If there's one truth I've carried through every bruise, betrayal, and breaking point, it's this:

If Black and Brown ever truly united, the world would never be the same.

That's not just a slogan—it's a prophecy. One I've felt in my bones since I was a kid. One I've dreamed of during every fight when I had to pick a side that didn't want me. One I know could save us all if we could only unlearn the lies we've been fed.

Because that's what this divide is—a lie. A carefully crafted illusion handed down through centuries of conquest, colonization, slavery, segregation, incarceration, and systemic control. Divide and conquer: the oldest trick in the book. And for far too long, we've been playing into it.

I've seen it with my own eyes—how Black and Brown folks walk the same streets, face the same poverty, breathe the same toxic air, eat the same poisonous food. How we bury our sons to the same gun violence. How we get pulled over, frisked, and funneled into the same prison cells. How we sit in the same underfunded schools with outdated books and overworked teachers.

We're living parallel lives. Just in different languages.

But instead of reaching for each other, too often we turn on each other.

And I get it. The roots are deep. Colorism runs through both cultures like poison in the bloodstream. In Latino communities, anti-Blackness is woven into the fabric—leftovers from colonization, reinforced by media that praises white skin and European features. Black folks, too, sometimes adopt the same superiority complex toward immigrants, shaped by survival in a country that pits marginalized people against one another for scraps.

I've seen Mexican kids scared to embrace their Afro-Latino heritage. I've seen Black kids dismiss Chicano culture as foreign. I've seen us beef over territory we don't even own, over flags we barely understand, over colors that can't hold the weight of our pain.

And all the while, the system wins.

Because when we fight each other, we forget who built the cages.

But imagine—just imagine—if we stopped.

Imagine if we looked past the skin tones and accents and recognized the shared trauma. If we said: *Your pain is my pain. Your story is my story. Your liberation is tied to mine.*

I've lived in the in-between my entire life. Half-Black. Half-Mexican. Rejected by both at different times but shaped by both in equal measure. I know the power that lives in this middle space. **It's not confusion—it's clarity. It's not conflict—it's connection.**

I've danced to Vicente Fernández and blasted LL Cool J. I've eaten tacos on Tuesday and fried chicken on Sunday. I've spoken Spanish with my Abuelita and coded my English on the block with other Black kids. **I've lived in two worlds. But I've never stopped dreaming of one.**

One where Brown hands lock with Black hands—not in fists, but in fists *raised together.*

One where we organize, educate, and rise—side by side—against a system that's always underestimated us both.

One where we don't just share culture—we share *purpose.*

I want that for our kids. I want that for our future. But we must name the wounds before we can heal them.

Mexican folks, we need to talk about anti-Blackness in our homes. About the jokes we let slide. The preferences we pass down. The words like *mayate and changuito*—that we say in front of our children, not realizing we're teaching them to hate their own people.

Black folks, we need to open the door wider. Acknowledge the pain our Brown brothers and sisters carry, especially in a system that criminalizes them too. We can't afford to gatekeep pain. We can't afford to build walls where we need bridges.

Because the truth is—we've both been exploited. Both been painted as criminals, animals, threats. We've both been redlined, underpaid, miseducated, and locked up. We've both lost leaders to assassination and movements to infiltration. We've both watched as our culture gets stolen, watered down, and resold to us at a markup.

And we've both survived.

Which means together?

We are unstoppable.

This is my love letter to both sides of my blood. To the Black kids who never felt welcome in Latino spaces. To the Brown kids who were told their Blackness was something to hide. To the biracial kids who've been straddling this line like I have, not knowing if they belong anywhere.

You do.

You belong to the future we're trying to build. One where we're not just coexisting—we're co-leading.

Imagine a movement where mariachi meets gospel. Where Cinco de Mayo joins Juneteenth. Where lowriders and Black Panthers march the same streets with the same chants. Where we stop asking, "What side are you on?" and start answering, "I'm on *our* side."

The world has always feared the day we'd wake up and realize we're family.

So, let's make their fear real.

Let's teach our kids that unity isn't soft—it's revolutionary. **That loving your culture doesn't mean hating someone else's.** That the system taught us to see each other as threats because it knew what we could be if we stood together.

Let's be that.

Let's be the dream they tried to bury...

Let's be the riot of love that breaks the silence...

Let's be the proof that Black and Brown don't just mix—they *multiply*.

Chapter 15:

LEGACY OF A DUAL-BLOODED MAN

L egacy is a strange thing.

When you grow up like I did—in shadows, fists, and silences—you start to wonder if you'll leave behind anything other than pain. You look at your lineage and see broken promises, missing fathers, bruised children, shattered women, and wonder, ***what will they say when I'm gone?***

For a long time, I thought my legacy would be rage.

I thought I'd pass down the same anger I inherited, the same silence I was forced into. I thought I'd become the man who scars instead of shelters, who repeats instead of reimagines. But something happened on the way to that future—I broke the cycle.

Not all at once. Not cleanly. But I broke it.

Piece by jagged piece, I chose to become something else. Something no man before me had been allowed to be... *healed.*

That is my legacy now.

Not perfection. Not some sanitized version of a survivor story. But truth. Vulnerability. Redemption.

I've learned that your blood doesn't define you—but how you carry it does.

Yes, I am Black. And I am Mexican. I am the child of contradiction, born from a union most people whispered about and many disrespected. But I've come to love every inch of that contradiction. I've come to see it not as a wound—but as a weapon. Not as a curse—but as a calling.

Because when you walk between worlds, you get to speak both languages. You get to translate pain into understanding. You get to become the bridge.

And we need bridges now more than ever.

When I look at the world today, I still see the divisions. I see Black and Brown kids fighting in prisons, schools and neighborhoods that neither of them owns. I see colorism still poisoning our mirrors, our families, our love. I see cycles repeating themselves in new packaging—same racism, new hashtags.

But I also see resistance.

I see Afro-Latinos reclaiming both sides of their story. I see mixed kids standing tall in their skin. I see Black and Brown organizers linking arms in the streets, saying, *not this time.* I see music, food, fashion, language—*culture*—blending in ways that honor rather than erase.

I see possibility.

I want my legacy rooted in that possibility.

And I'll keep telling the truth—about my mother, about Rock, about Sid, about myself—not because I want pity, but because I want freedom. You can't be free from what you refuse to face. And **I want freedom not just for me, but**

for every kid out there caught in the middle, thinking their story has no place in this world.

It does...

***You* do.**

This book, this testimony, this journey—it isn't just about me. It's about all of us. The ones who were born into two cultures, two struggles, two tongues, and were told we had to choose.

We don't.... We are allowed to be both.

We are allowed to break and rebuild...

We are allowed to grieve our pain and still claim our joy...

We are allowed to burn down what hurt us and grow gardens in its place...

My name is *James* and *Jaime.*

I am the son of Esperanza, a child of pain and survival, a man raised in fists who now lives with open hands.

I am Black...

I am Mexican...

I am not a statistic...

I am not a mistake...

I am a legacy in motion...

And if you're reading this—if you've made it this far—it means you are a part of it also.

So here is my final truth:

Unity is not a dream. It's Love. It's a decision.

And I've made mine.

James Bass / Jaime Basillo

www.ingramcontent.com/pod-product-compliance
Lightning Source LLC
Chambersburg PA
CBRC101141030426
42335CB00007B/200